KIDS' BROADWAY SONGBOOK

SONGS ORIGINALLY SUNG ON STAGE BY CHILDREN

CONTENTS

ANNIE	2	It's the Hard-Knock Li
	6	Maybe
	8	Tomorrow
GYPSY	11	Let Me Entertain You
	14	Little Lamb
THE KING AND I	20	I Whistle a Happy Tune
MAME	24	My Best Girl
THE ME NOBODY KNOWS	26	The Tree
LES MISÉRABLES	17	Castle on a Cloud
THE MUSIC MAN	29	Gary, Indiana
OLIVER!	32	Where Is Love?
	34	Who Will Buy?
PETER PAN	38	I Won't Grow Up
	42	Wendy
THE SECRET GARDEN	45	The Girl I Mean to Be
	48	Round-Shouldered Man
SHENANDOAH	56	Why Am I Me?
SOUTH PACIFIC	54	Dites-Moi (Tell Me Why)

D1495829

Hal Leonard Publishing Corporation

7777 West Bluemound Road P.O. Box 13819 Milwaukee, WI 53213

IT'S THE HARD-KNOCK LIFE

from ANNIE

Lyric by MARTIN CHARNIN
Music by CHARLES STROUSE

MAYBE
from ANNIE

Lyric by MARTIN CHARNIN
Music by CHARLES STROUSE

Tenderly

May - be far a - way, Or may-be real near - by,
May - be in a house all hid-den by a hill,

He may be pour-ing her cof - fee, She may be straight-'ning his tie.
She's sit - ting play-ing pi - a - nah,

He's sit - ting pay-ing a bill. Bet-cha they're young,— Bet-cha they're smart,—
Bet-cha he reads,— Bet-cha she sews,—

Bet they col-lect things like   ash trays and art.___ Bet-cha they're good___ why should-n't they be,___
May-be she's made me a   clos-et of clothes.___ May-be they're strict___As straight as a line,___

Their one mis-take was   giv-ing up me.___ So,   may-be now it's   time,   and
Don't real-ly care as   long as they're mine.___ So,   may-be now this prayer's   the

may-be when I   wake   They'll be there call-ing me   "Ba — by,"   May —
last one of it's   kind;   Won't you please come get your   ba — by,

be.   May — be.

TOMORROW
from ANNIE

Lyric by MARTIN CHARNIN
Music by CHARLES STROUSE

The sun-'ll come out ___ to-mor-row, bet your bot-tom dol-lar that to-mor-row ___ there'll be sun! Jus' think-ing a-bout ___ to-mor-row clears a-way the cob-webs and the sor-row ___ till there's none. When I'm stuck with a

LET ME ENTERTAIN YOU

from GYPSY

Words by STEPHEN SONDHEIM
Music by JULE STYNE

LITTLE LAMB
from GYPSY

Words by STEPHEN SONDHEIM
Music by JULE STYNE

CASTLE ON A CLOUD
from LES MISERABLES

Music by CLAUDE-MICHEL SCHÖNBERG
Lyrics by HERBERT KRETZMER
Original Text by ALAIN BOUBLIL and JEAN-MARC NATEL

There is a cas - tle on a cloud.
There is a room that's full of toys.

I like to go there in my sleep.
There are a hun - dred boys and girls.

says, "Co-sette, I love you ver-y much." I know a place where no-one's

lost. I know a place where no-one

cries. Cry - ing at all is not al -

lowed, not in my cas - tle on a cloud.

I WHISTLE A HAPPY TUNE
from THE KING AND I

Lyrics by OSCAR HAMMERSTEIN II
Music by RICHARD RODGERS

22

MY BEST GIRL

(MY BEST BEAU)
from MAME

Music and Lyric by
JERRY HERMAN

THE TREE
from THE ME NOBODY KNOWS

Lyric by WILL HOLT
Music by GARY WILLIAM FRIEDMAN

GARY, INDIANA
from Meredith Willson's THE MUSIC MAN

By MEREDITH WILLSON

Soft Shoe Bounce

Piano

Voice

Ga-ry, In-di-an - a, Ga-ry, In-di-an - a, Ga-ry, In-di-

an - a, let me say it once a-gain.

Ga-ry, In-di-an - a, Ga-ry, In-di-an - a, Ga-ry, In-di-

WHERE IS LOVE?
from the Columbia Pictures-Romulus film OLIVER!

Words and Music by
LIONEL BART

Slowly, but rhythmically

WHO WILL BUY?

from the Columbia Pictures-Romulus film OLIVER!

Words and Music by
LIONEL BART

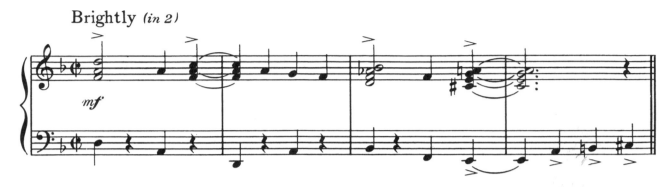

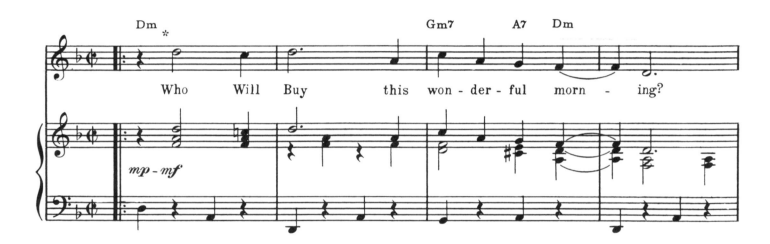

Who Will Buy this won-der-ful morn - ing?

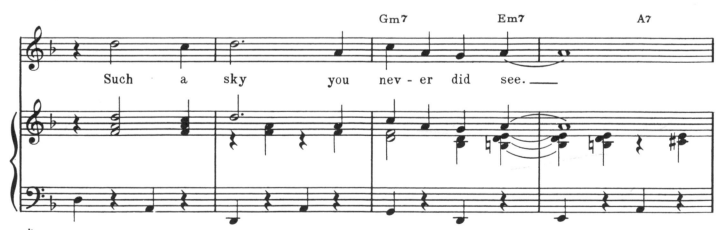

Such a sky you nev-er did see. ___

*After additional lyrics following 2nd ending, sing these words to above music marked *:
Who will buy this wonderful feeling? I'm so high I swear I could fly! What a sky! A heavenly ceiling, Inviting you to come and buy!

† *Additional film lyrics following 2nd ending: (Sing to music marked†)*
Who will buy this morning of mornings? Makes you feel you're walking on air. Ev'ry tree and flower is singing, "How fortunate are we to be alive to see, The dawning of a day so fair!"

I WON'T GROW UP

from PETER PAN

Lyric by CAROLYN LEIGH
Music by MARK CHARLAP

WENDY
from PETER PAN

Lyric by BETTY COMDEN and ADOLPH GREEN
Music by JULE STYNE

THE GIRL I MEAN TO BE
from THE SECRET GARDEN

Lyrics by MARSHA NORMAN
Music by LUCY SIMON

Piano arrangement by Michael Kosarin

ROUND-SHOULDERED MAN
from THE SECRET GARDEN

Lyrics by MARSHA NORMAN
Music by LUCY SIMON

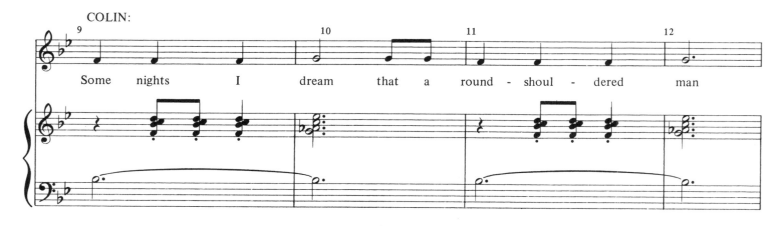

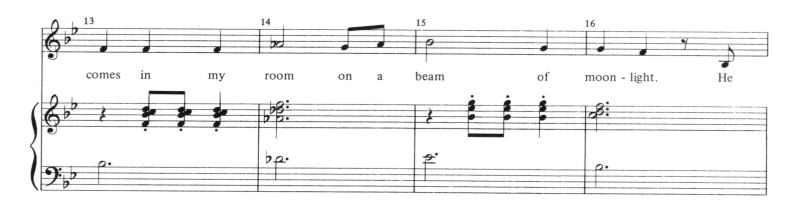

Piano Arrangement by Michael Kosarin

sits with a book in his hands.

And then I dreamed that the round - shoul - dered man takes me

sempre legato

off on a ride through the moors by moon - light He

nev - er says where we'll go, we just

all that's good and true.

And once I dreamed that the round - shoul - dered man took my

hand, and we walked to a se - cret gar - den. I

DITES-MOI (TELL ME WHY)

from SOUTH PACIFIC

Lyrics by OSCAR HAMMERSTEIN II
Music by RICHARD RODGERS

WHY AM I ME?
from SHENANDOAH

Lyric by PETER UDELL
Music by GARY GELD

Brightly

Tell ya what I'm think-in', hon-est-ly and true. How
Lord, I know the feel-in', 'cause when I'm by my-self I

come I come to life as me and not to life as you?
won-der why I'm who I am and not some-bod-y

some - bod - y puts___ the "who" in - to folks___ like drop - pin' a stone___ in a lake.___

(simile)

So may - be I'm think - in' I'm A - bra-ham Lin - coln and

some - bod - y made___ a mis - take! If I were

MUSICAL THEATRE COLLECTIONS
FROM HAL LEONARD

BROADWAY BELTER'S SONGBOOK

A great new collection for women singers. All the songs have been chosen especially for this type of voice, and the ranges and keys have been carefully selected. 30 songs, including: Broadway Baby • The Lady Is A Tramp • Everything's Coming Up Roses • I'd Give My Life To You (*Miss Saigon*) • Cabaret. 176 pages.
_____00311608 ....$16.95

THE SINGER'S MUSICAL THEATRE ANTHOLOGY

The most comprehensive collection of Broadway selections ever organized specifically for the singer. Each of the five volumes contains important songs chosen because of their appropriateness to that particular voice type. All selections are in their authentic form, excerpted from the original vocal scores. The songs in *The Singer's Musical Theatre Anthology*, written by such noted composers as Kurt Weill, Richard Rodgers, Stephen Sondheim, and Jerome Kern, are vocal masterpieces ideal for the auditioning, practicing or performing vocalist.

Soprano

46 songs, including: Where Or When • If I Loved You • Goodnight, My Someone • Smoke Gets In Your Eyes • Barbara Song • and many more.
_____00361071 ....$17.95

Mezzo-Soprano/Alto

40 songs, including: My Funny Valentine • I Love Paris • Don't Cry For Me Argentina • Losing My Mind • Send In The Clowns • and many more.
_____00361072 ....$17.95

Tenor

42 songs, including: Stranger In Paradise • On The Street Where You Live • Younger Than Springtime • Lonely House • Not While I'm Around • and more.
_____00361073 ....$17.95

Baritone/Bass

37 songs, including: If Ever I Would Leave You • September Song • The Impossible Dream • Ol' Man River • Some Enchanted Evening • and more.
_____00361074 ....$17.95

Duets

21 songs, including: Too Many Mornings • We Kiss In A Shadow • People Will Say We're In Love • Bess You Is My Woman • Make Believe • more.
_____00361075 ....$14.95

THE SINGER'S MUSICAL THEATRE ANTHOLOGY VOL. 2

More great theatre songs for singers in a continuation of this highly successful and important series, once again compiled and edited by Richard Walters. As is the case with the first volume, these collections are as valuable to the classical singer as they are to the popular and theatre performer.

Soprano, Volume 2

42 songs, including: All Through The Night • And This Is My Beloved • Vilia • If I Were A Bell • Think Of Me.
_____00747030 ....$18.95

Mezzo-Soprano/Alto, Volume 2

44 songs, including: If He Walked Into My Life • The Party's Over • Johnny One Note • Adalaide's Lament • I Hate Men • I Dreamed A Dream.
_____00747031 ....$18.95

Tenor, Volume 2

46 songs, including: Miracle Of Miracles • Sit Down, You're Rockin' The Boat • Giants In The Sky • Bring Him Home • Music Of The Night.
_____00747032 ....$18.95

Baritone/Bass, Volume 2

44 songs, including: Guido's Song from *Nine* • Bye, Bye Baby • I Won't Send Roses • The Surrey With The Fringe On Top • Once In Love With Amy.
_____00747033 ....$18.95

THE ACTOR'S SONGBOOK

A wonderfully diverse collection of comedy songs, character songs, Vaudeville numbers, dramatic songs, and ballads for the actor who sings. A perfect resource to use for finding an audition song or specialty number. In two editions, one for women, and one for men, with a completely different selection of songs chosen for each edition. Over 50 songs in each book. Women's edition titles include: The Ladies Who Lunch • Cla-wence (Don't Tweat Me So Wough) • Cry Me A River • Shy • The Man That Got Away, and many more. Men's edition includes: Buddy's Blues (from *Follies*) • Doing The Reactionary • How to Handle A Woman • I'm Calm • Reviewing The Situation, many more.
_____00747035 Women's Edition $18.95
_____00747034 Men's Edition $18.95

HL For more information, see your local music dealer, or write to:
Hal Leonard Publishing Corporation
P.O. Box 13819 Milwaukee, Wisconsin 53213
Prices, contents and availability subject to change without notice.

KIDS' BROADWAY SONGBOOK

An unprecedented collection of songs that were originally performed by children on the Broadway stage. A terrific and much needed publication for the thousands of children studying voice. Includes 16 songs for boys and girls: Gary, Indiana (*The Music Man*) • Castle On A Cloud (*Les Miserables*) • Where Is Love? (*Oliver!*) • Tomorrow (*Annie*) • and more.
_____00311609 ....$8.95

MUSICAL THEATRE CLASSICS

A fantastic series featuring the best songs from Broadway classics. Collections are organized by voice type and each book includes recorded piano accompaniments on cassette – ideal for practicing. Compiled by Richard Walters, Sue Malmberg, pianist.

Soprano, Volume 1

13 songs, including: Climb Ev'ry Mountain • Falling In Love With Love • Hello, Young Lovers • Smoke Gets In Your Eyes • Wishing You Were Somehow Here Again.
_____00660148 ....$14.95

Soprano, Volume 2

13 more favorites, including: Can't Help Lovin' Dat Man • I Could Have Danced All Night • Show Me • Think Of Me • Till There Was You.
_____00660149 ....$14.95

Mezzo-Soprano/Alto, Volume 1

12 songs, including: Don't Cry For Me Argentina • I Dreamed A Dream • The Lady Is A Tramp • People • and more.
_____00660150 ....$14.95

Mezzo-Soprano/Alto, Volume 2

12 songs, including: Glad To Be Unhappy • Just You Wait • Memory • My Funny Valentine • On My Own • and more.
_____00660151 ....$14.95

Tenor

12 songs, including: All I Need Is A Girl • If You Could See Her • The Music Of The Night • On The Street Where You Live • Younger Than Springtime • and more.
_____00660152 ....$14.95

Baritone/Bass

10 classics, including: If Ever I Would Leave You • If I Loved You • Oh, What A Beautiful Mornin' • Ol' Man River • Try To Remember • and more.
_____00660153 ....$14.95